MOTOWN HITS

CONTENTS

T0039491

2 AIN'T NO MOUNTAIN HIGH ENOUGH

7 AIN'T NOTHING LIKE THE REAL THING

10 ALL IN LOVE IS FAIR

14 BABY I NEED YOUR LOVIN'

17 BEN

20 EASY

28 HOW SWEET IT IS (TO BE LOVED BY YOU)

25 I BELIEVE (WHEN I FALL IN LOVE IT WILL BE FOREVER)

32 I CAN'T HELP MYSELF (SUGAR PIE, HONEY BUNCH)

36 I HEARD IT THROUGH THE GRAPEVINE

40 ISN'T SHE LOVELY

44 MY CHERIE AMOUR

47 SHOP AROUND

52 SINCE I LOST MY BABY

56 THREE TIMES A LADY

61 TOO HIGH

66 YOU ARE THE SUNSHINE OF MY LIFE

70 YOU CAN'T HURRY LOVE

— PIANO LEVEL —
LATE INTERMEDIATE/
EARLY ADVANCED

ISBN- 978-1-4234-0791-1

HAL•LEONARD®
CORPORATION
7777 W. BLUEMOUND RD. P.O. BOX 13819 MILWAUKEE, WI 53213

Visit Hal Leonard Online at
www.halleonard.com

Visit Phillip at
www.phillipkeveren.com

AIN'T NO MOUNTAIN HIGH ENOUGH

Words and Music by NICKOLAS ASHFORD
and VALERIE SIMPSON
Arranged by Phillip Keveren

Flowing smoothly (♩ = 126)

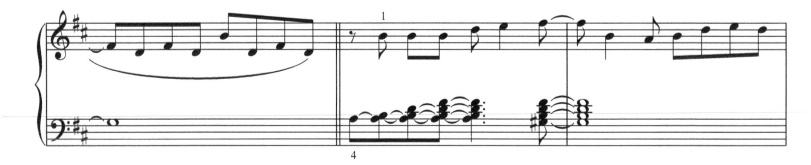

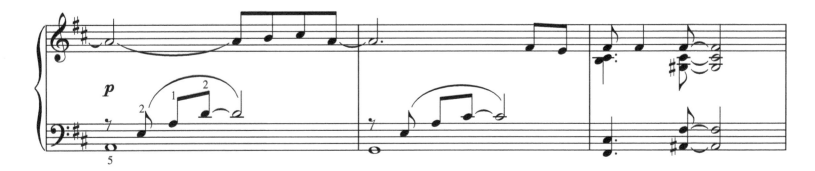

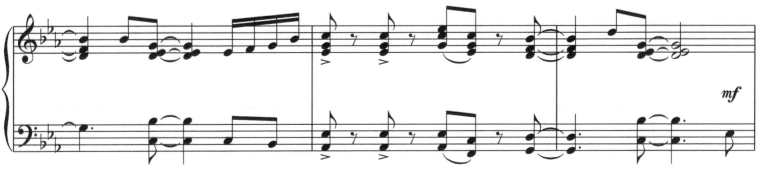

AIN'T NOTHING LIKE THE REAL THING

Words and Music by NICKOLAS ASHFORD
and VALERIE SIMPSON
Arranged by Phillip Keveren

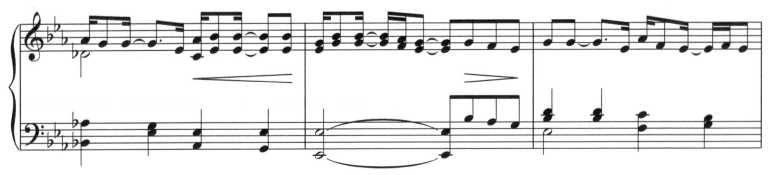

ALL IN LOVE IS FAIR

Words and Music by STEVIE WONDER
Arranged by Phillip Keveren

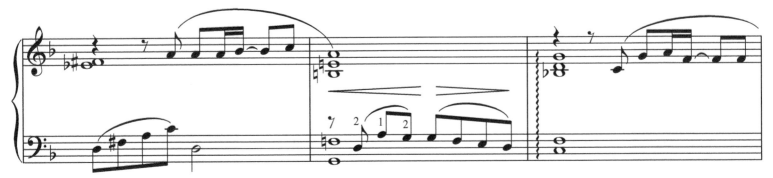

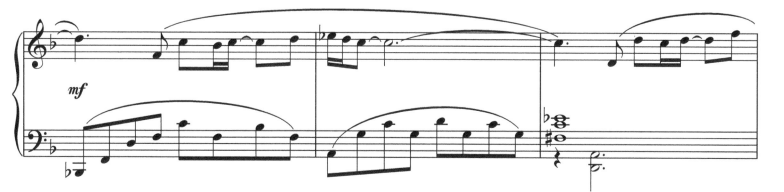

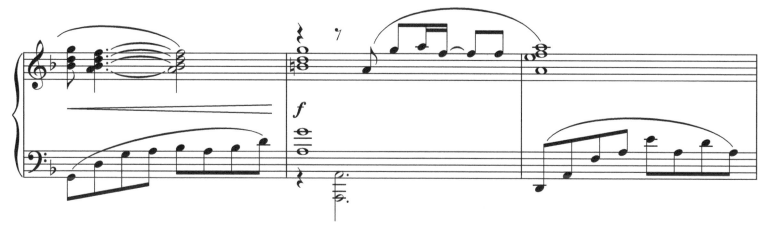

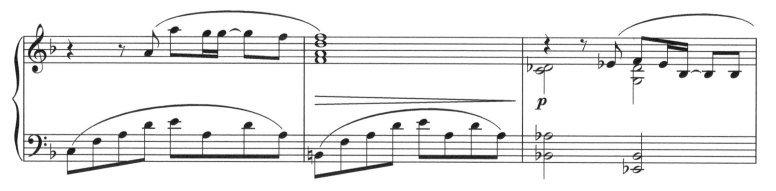

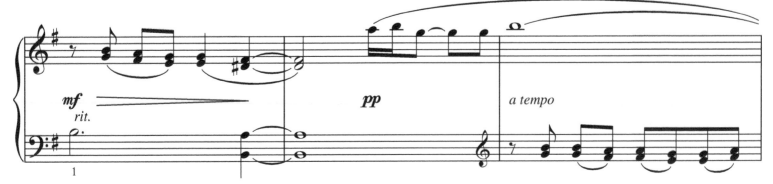

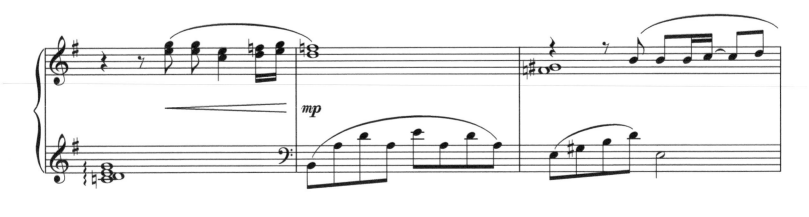

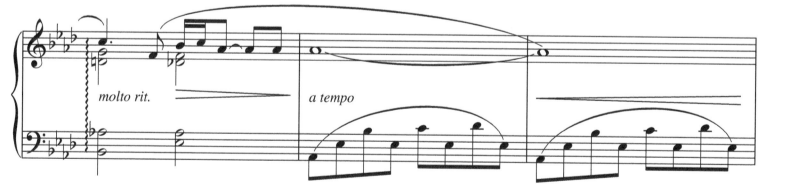

BABY I NEED YOUR LOVIN'

Words and Music by BRIAN HOLLAND,
LAMONT DOZIER and EDWARD HOLLAND
Arranged by Phillip Keveren

Moderate Rock (♩ = 120)

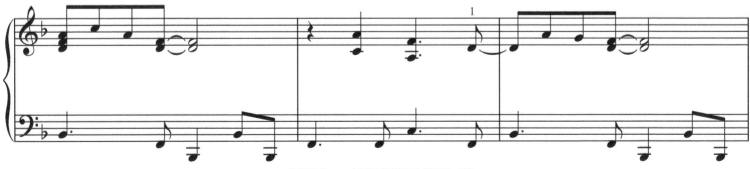

BEN

Words by DON BLACK
Music by WALTER SCHARF
Arranged by Phillip Keveren

Gently (♩ = 88)

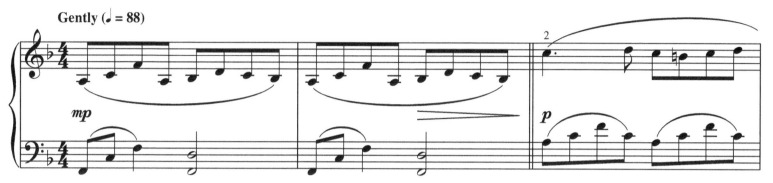

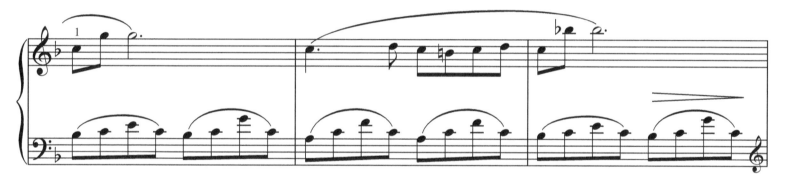

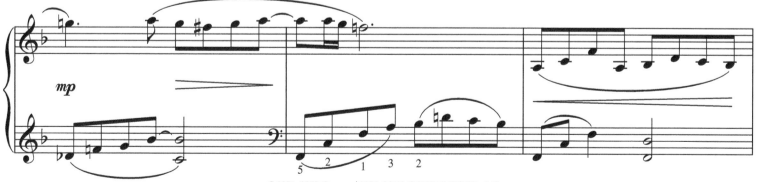

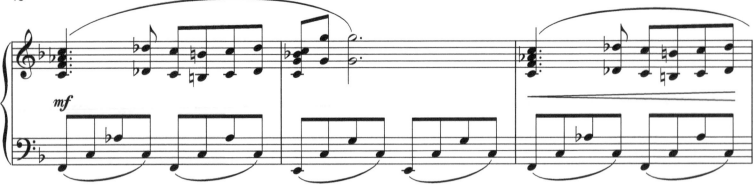

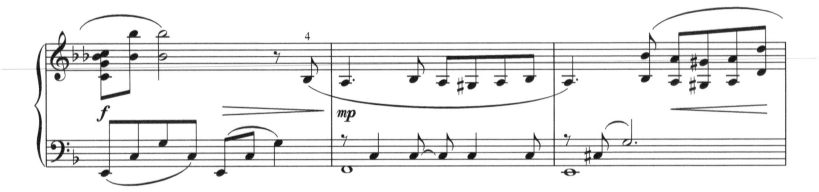

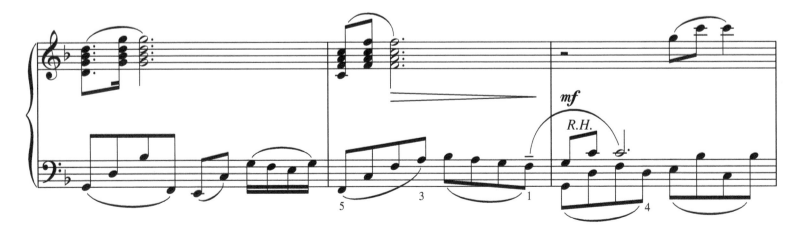

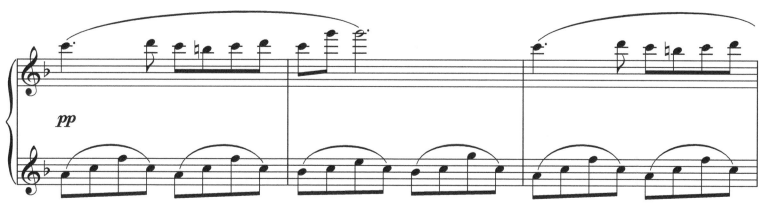

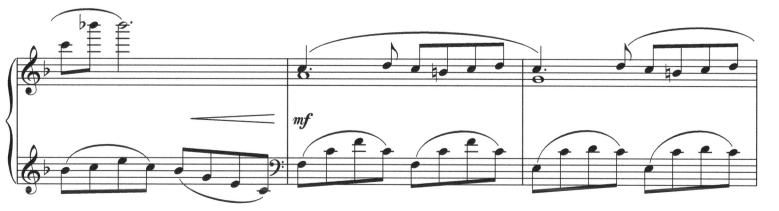

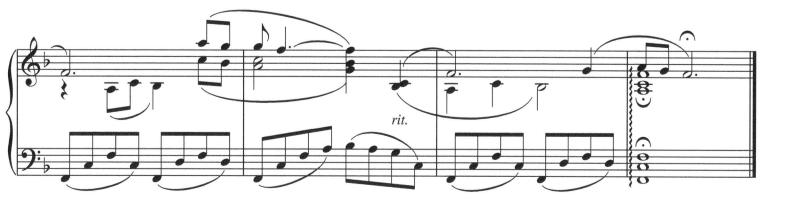

EASY

Words and Music by LIONEL RICHIE
Arranged by Phillip Keveren

Relaxed (♩ = 69) (16th-note Shuffle)

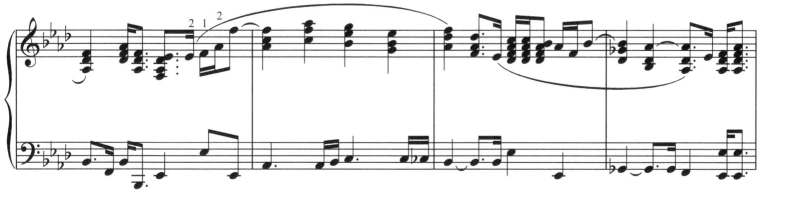

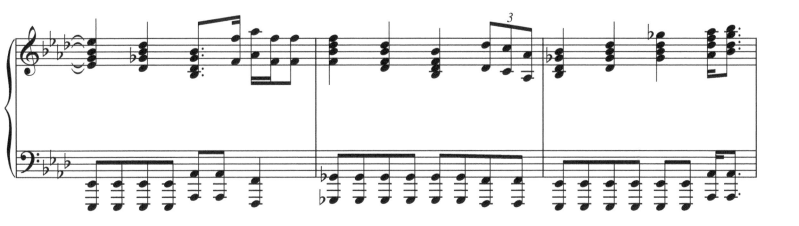

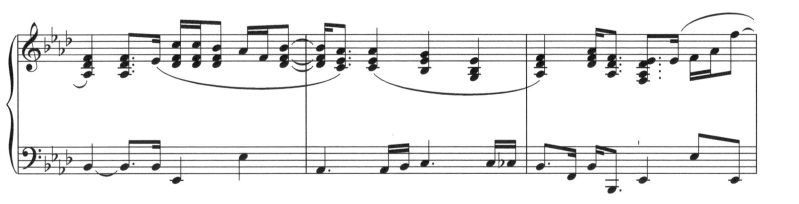

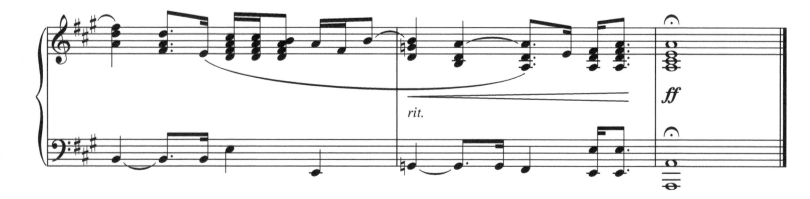

I BELIEVE
(When I Fall in Love It Will Be Forever)

Words and Music by STEVIE WONDER
and YVONNE WRIGHT
Arranged by Phillip Keveren

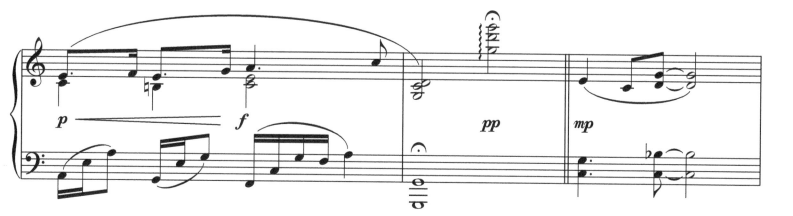

HOW SWEET IT IS
(To Be Loved by You)

Words and Music by EDWARD HOLLAND,
LAMONT DOZIER and BRIAN HOLLAND
Arranged by Phillip Keveren

Moderate Shuffle (♩ = 96–104)

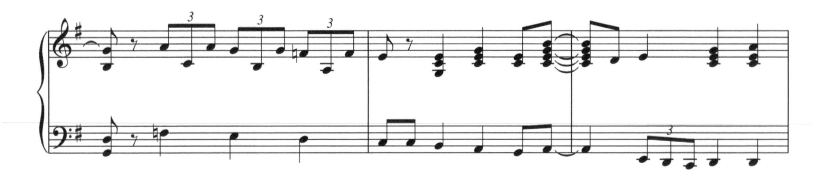

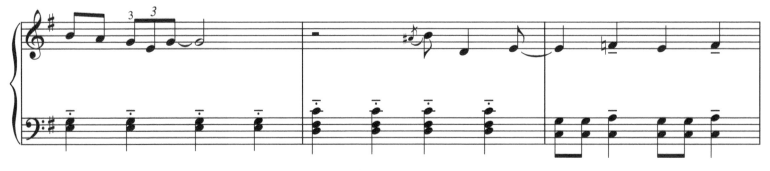

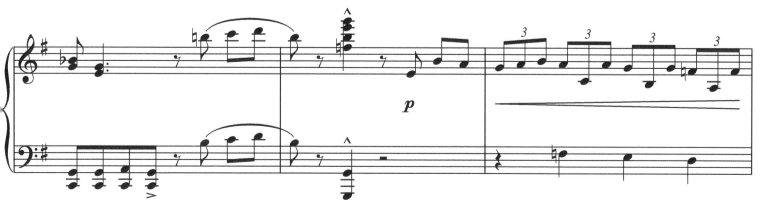

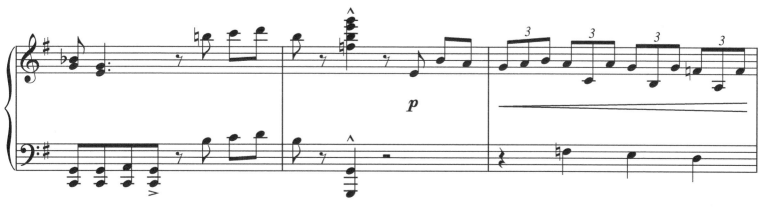

I CAN'T HELP MYSELF
(Sugar Pie, Honey Bunch)

Words and Music by BRIAN HOLLAND,
LAMONT DOZIER and EDWARD HOLLAND
Arranged by Phillip Keveren

Moderate Rock (♩ = 132)

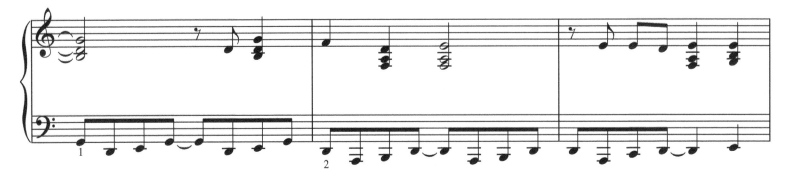

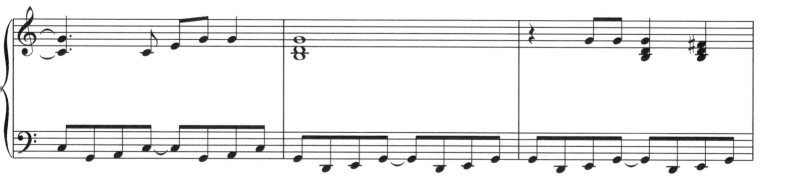

To Coda

D.S. al Coda

CODA

f

I HEARD IT THROUGH THE GRAPEVINE

Words and Music by NORMAN J. WHITFIELD
and BARRETT STRONG
Arranged by Phillip Keveren

Soulfully (♩ = 116)

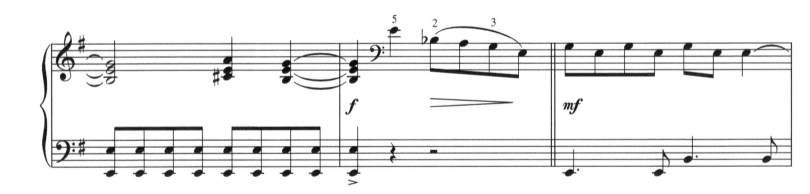

ISN'T SHE LOVELY

Words and Music by STEVIE WONDER
Arranged by Phillip Keveren

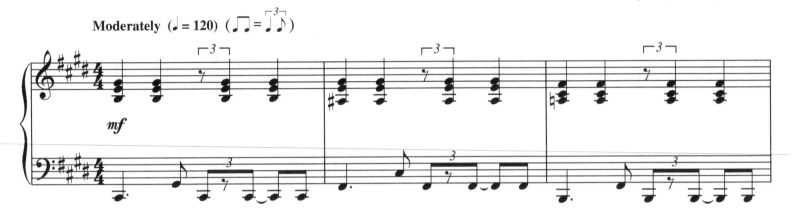

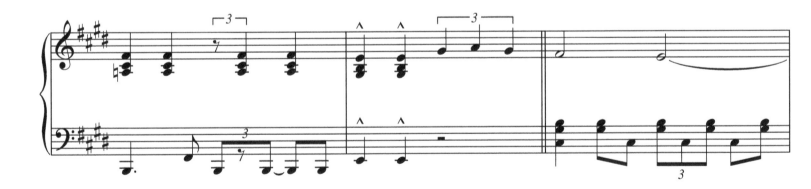

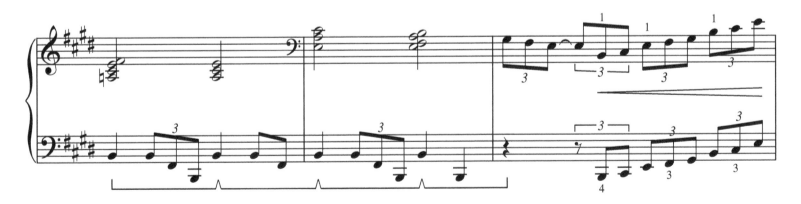

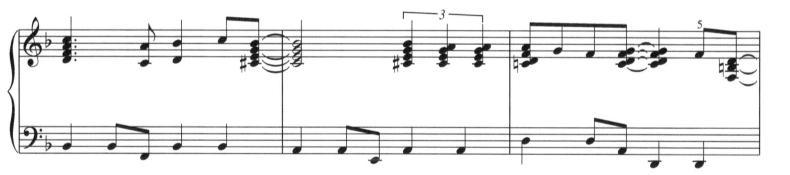

MY CHERIE AMOUR

Words and Music by STEVIE WONDER,
SYLVIA MOY and HENRY COSBY
Arranged by Phillip Keveren

Moderately ($\quad$ = 126)

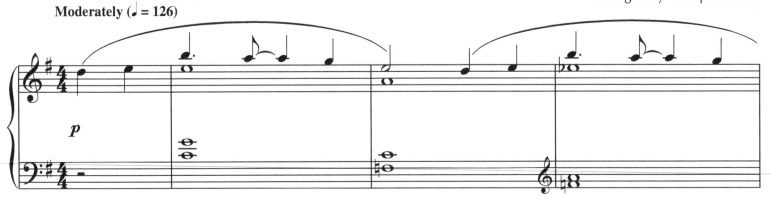

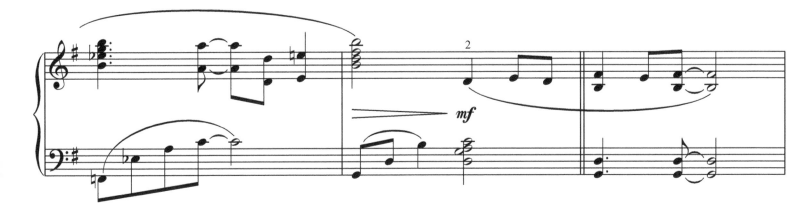

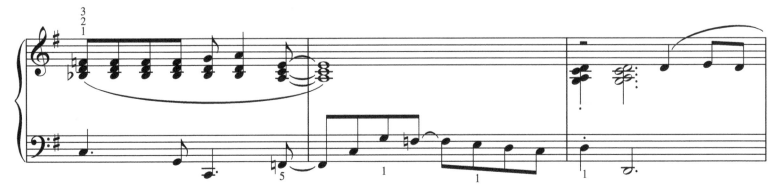

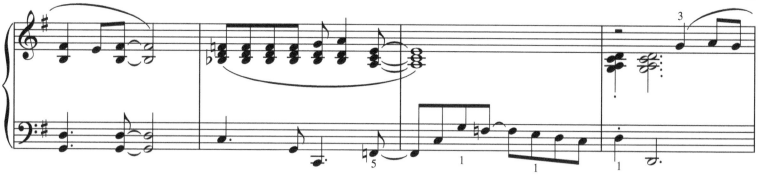

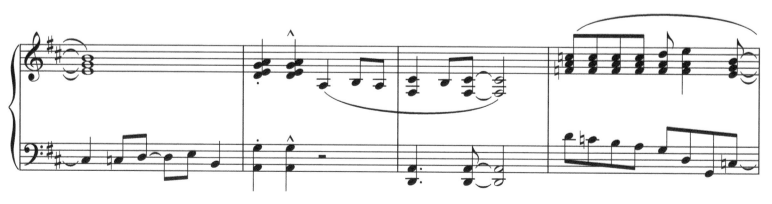

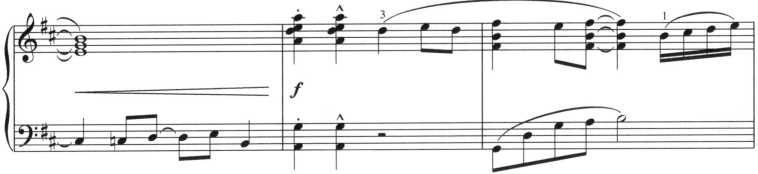

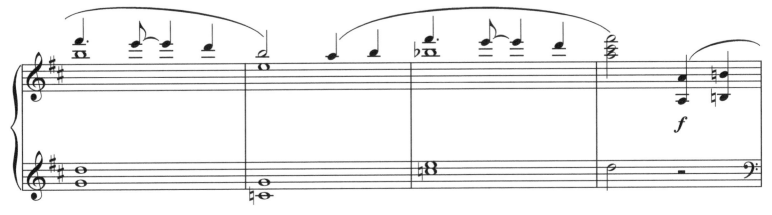

SHOP AROUND

Words and Music by BERRY GORDY
and WILLIAM "SMOKEY" ROBINSON
Arranged by Phillip Keveren

Medium Rock 'n' Roll ($\quad$ = 144)

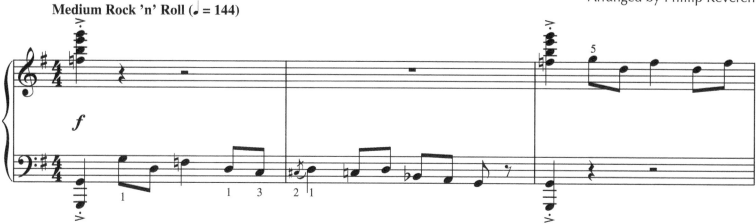

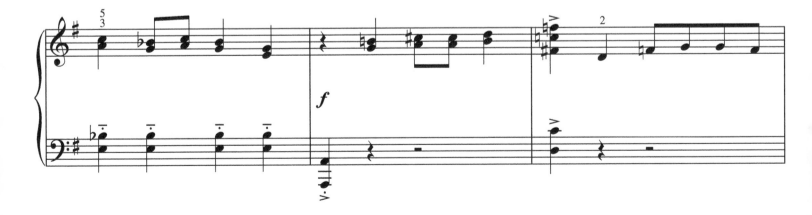

SINCE I LOST MY BABY

Words and Music by WILLIAM ROBINSON, JR.
and WARREN MOORE
Arranged by Phillip Keveren

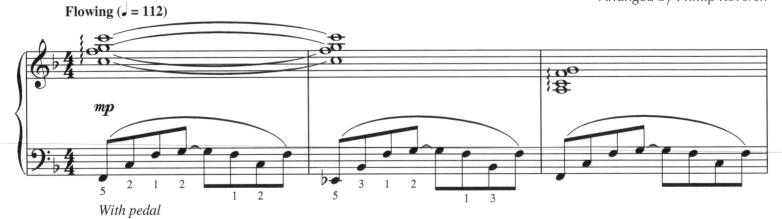

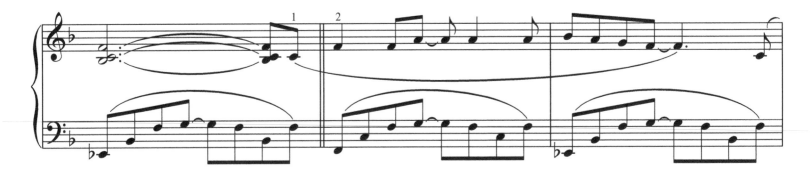

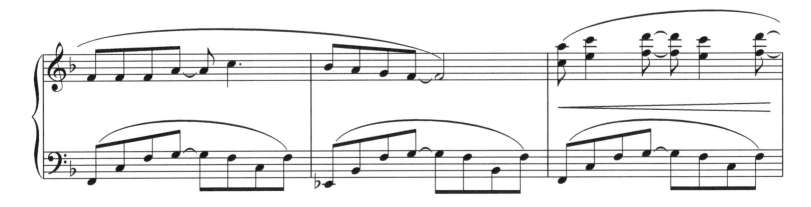

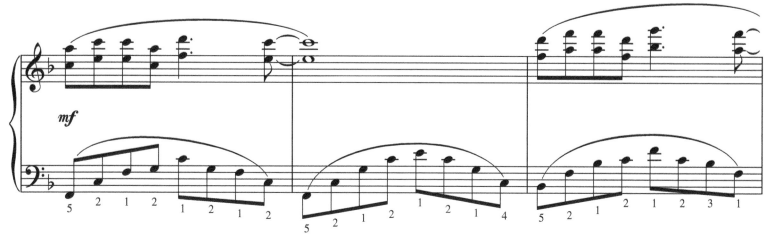

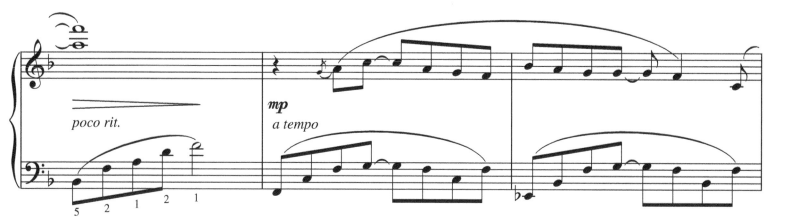

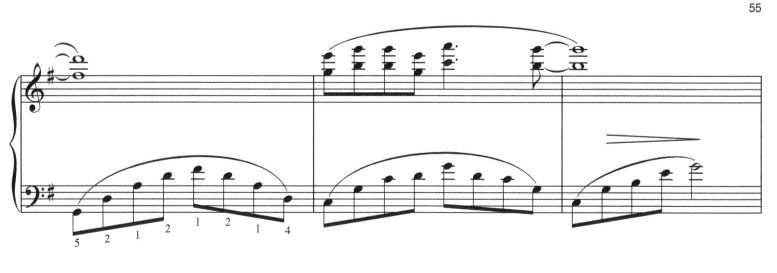

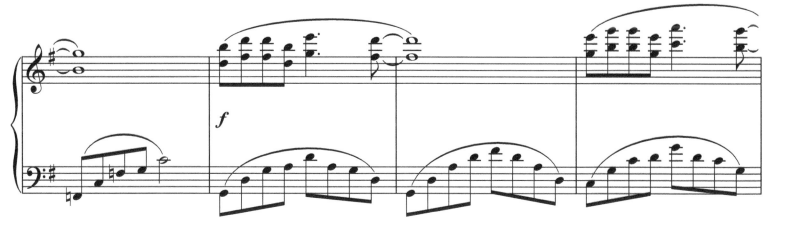

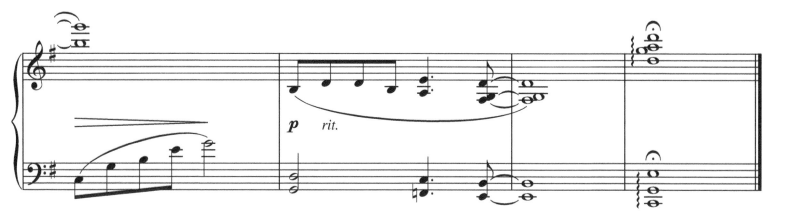

THREE TIMES A LADY

Words and Music by LIONEL RICHIE
Arranged by Phillip Keveren

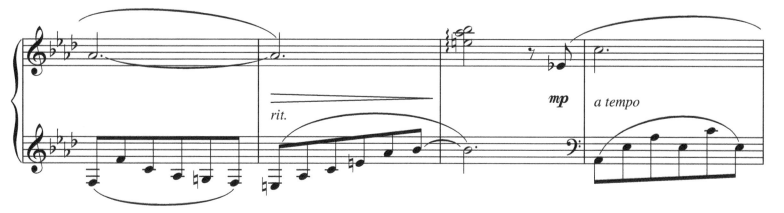

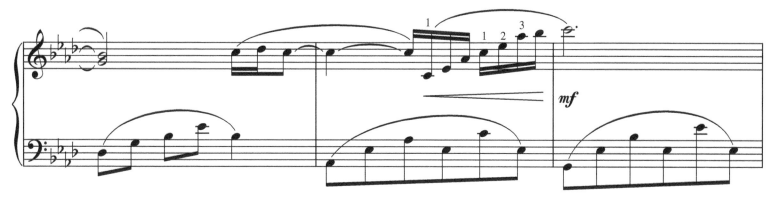

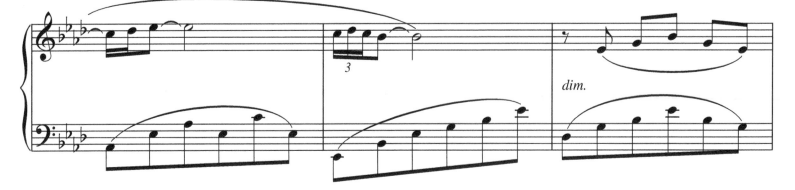

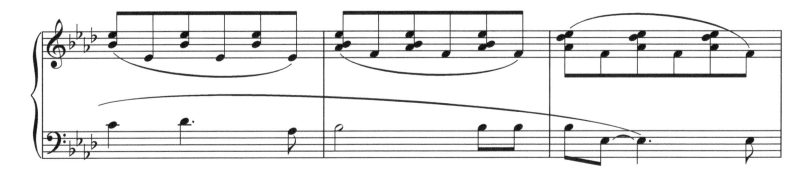

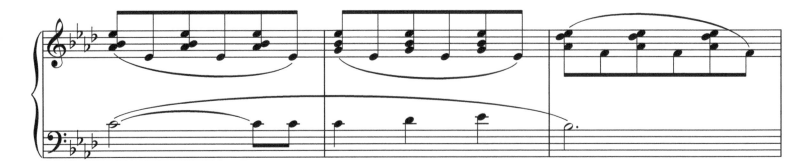

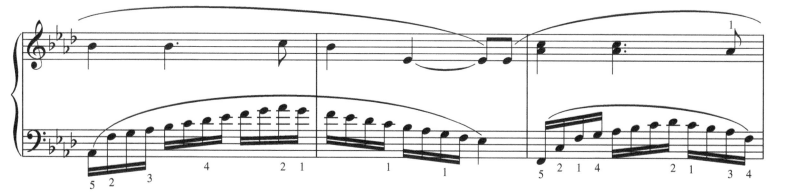

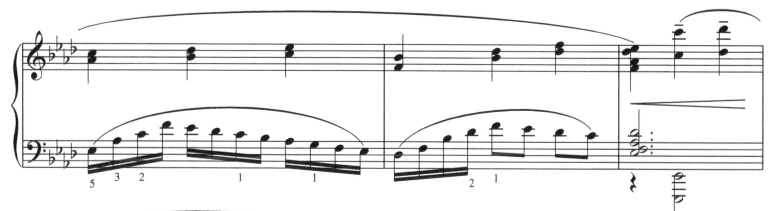

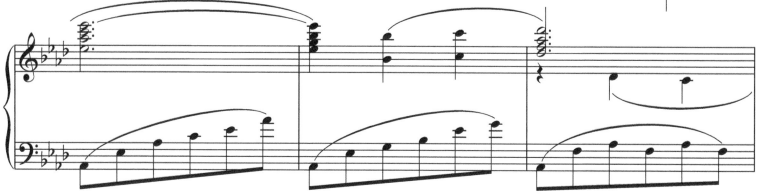

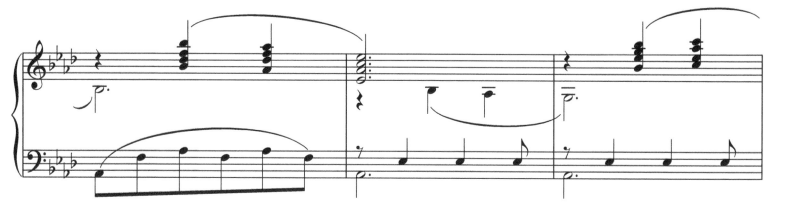

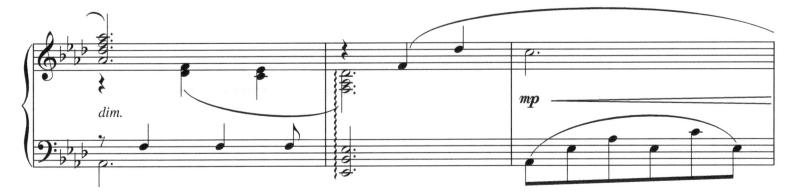

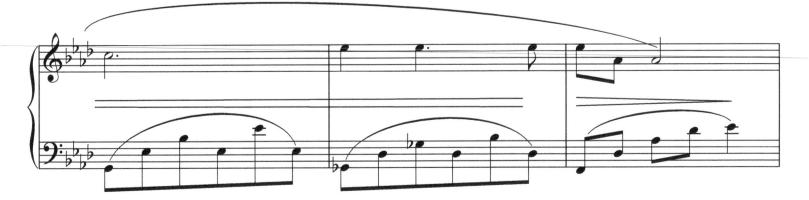

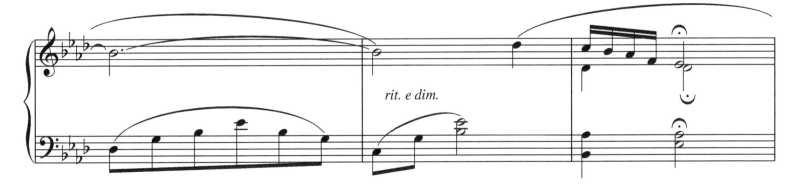

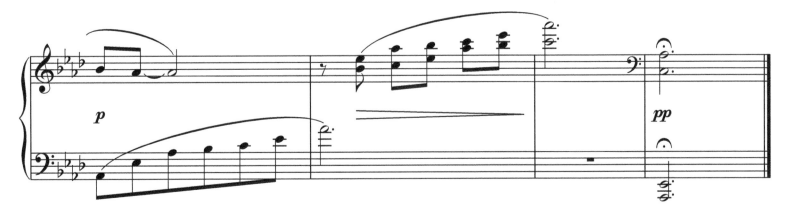

TOO HIGH

Words and Music by STEVIE WONDER
Arranged by Phillip Keveren

Medium Funk Shuffle (♩ = 96)

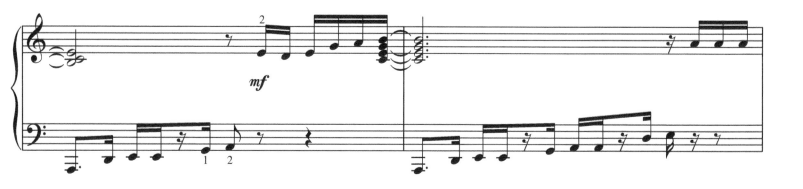

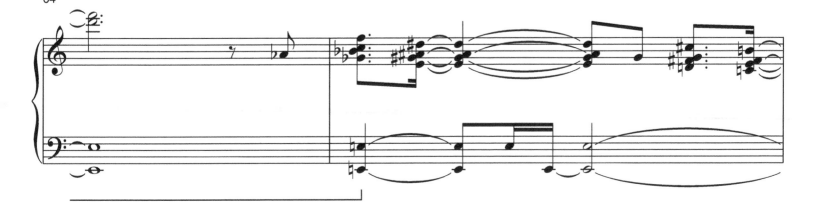

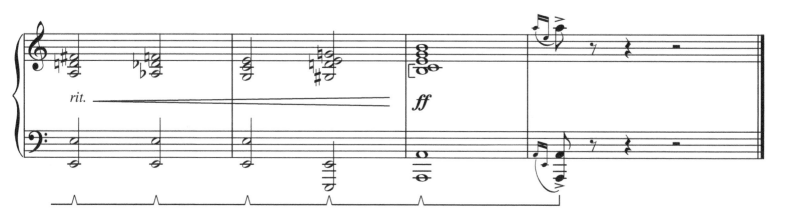

YOU ARE THE SUNSHINE OF MY LIFE

Words and Music by STEVIE WONDER
Arranged by Phillip Keveren

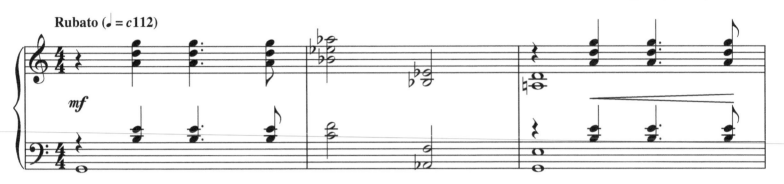

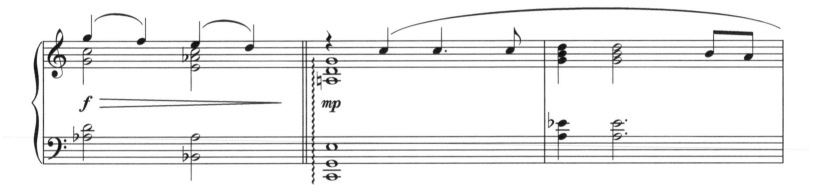

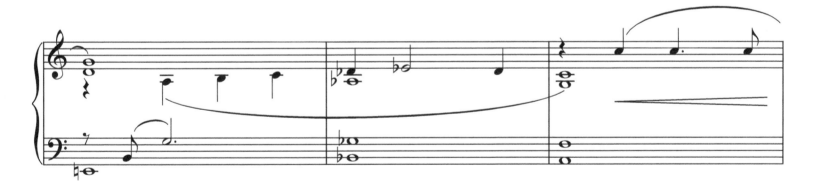

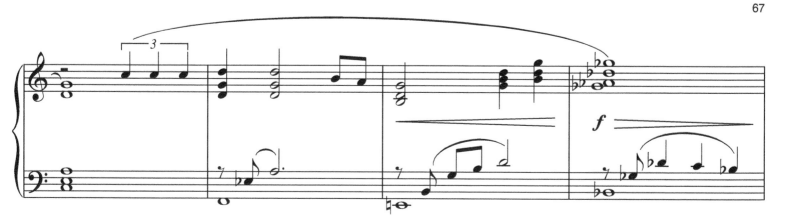

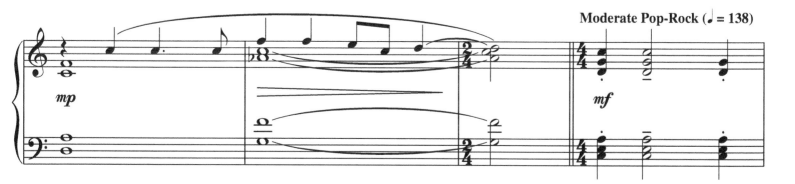

Moderate Pop-Rock (♩ = 138)

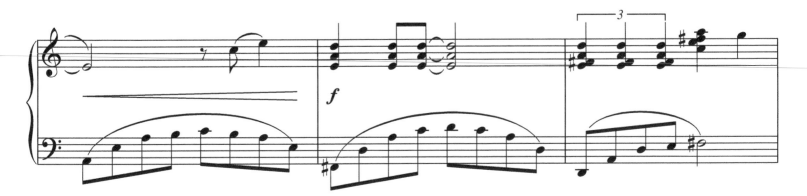

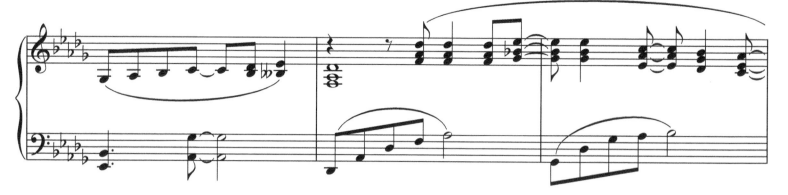

Rubato

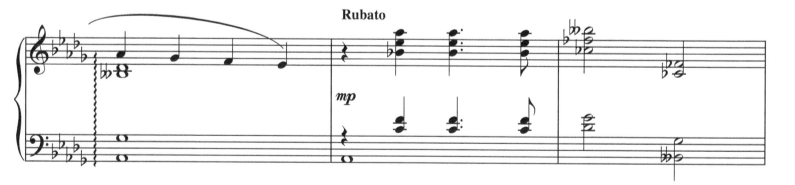

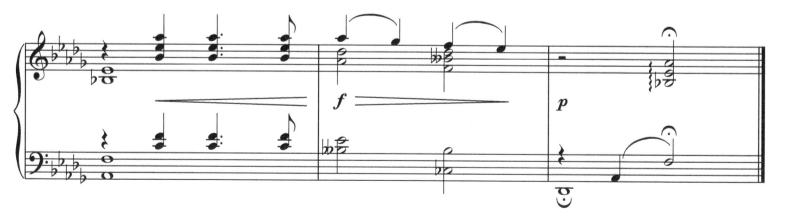

YOU CAN'T HURRY LOVE

Words and Music by EDWARD HOLLAND,
LAMONT DOZIER and BRIAN HOLLAND
Arranged by Phillip Keveren

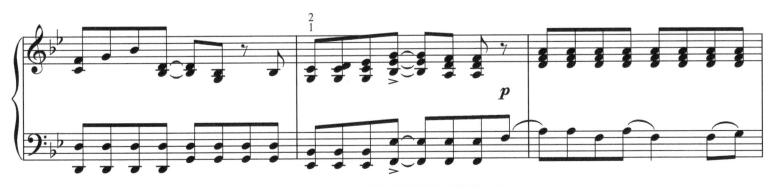

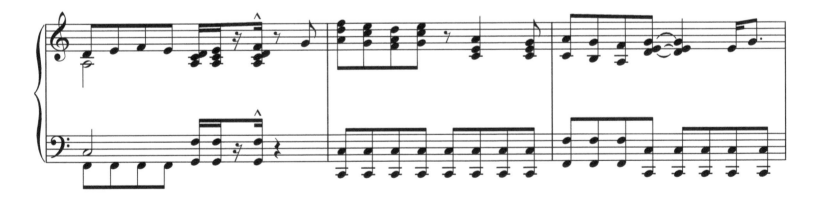